T0017420

Instructions
between
Takeoff
and
Landing

AKRON SERIES IN POETRY

Titles published since 2012.
For a complete listing of titles published in the series,
go to www.uakron.edu/uapress/poetry.

Instructions

between

Takeoff

and

Landing

Charles Jensen

The University of Akron Press
Akron, Ohio

ISBN: 978-1-62922-224-0 (paper)
ISBN: 978-1-62922-225-7 (ePDF)
ISBN: 978-1-62922-226-4 (ePub)

A catalog record for this title is available from the Library of Congress.

∞ The paper used in this publication meets the minimum requirements of ANSI/NISO z39.48–1992
(Permanence of Paper).

Cover image: *Skydiver* by Nathan Adkins, © 2019. Used with permission.
Cover design by Amy Freels.

Instructions between Takeoff and Landing was designed and typeset in Garamond with Avenir titles by
Amy Freels and printed on sixty-pound natural and bound by Bookmasters of Ashland, Ohio.

Produced in conjunction with the University
of Akron Affordable Learning Initiative.
More information is available at
www.uakron.edu/affordablelearning/.

for my brothers

Gary and Dennis
sailing on ahead

Contents

"Arriving at each new city, the traveler finds again a past of his that he did not know he had: the foreignness of what you no longer are or no longer possess lies in wait for you in foreign, unpossessed places."

—Italo Calvino, *Invisible Cities*

I.
ATMOSPHERIC
CONDITIONS

POEM IN WHICH WORDS HAVE BEEN LEFT OUT

—After the Miranda Rights, established 1966

You have the right to remain
anything you can and will be.

An attorney you cannot afford will
be provided to you.

You have silent will.
You can be against law.
You cannot afford one.

You remain silent. Anything you say
will be provided to you.

The right can and will be
against you. Have anything you say
be right. Anything you say
can be right. The right remain silent.

You will be held. You will be
provided. You cannot be you.

A STRANGER ASKS WHERE I AM FROM

1. Biographical

A forest atop a moraine;
a town inside the forest;
a house made of bricks;
a room from which I could not escape.

2. Mythological

A beast without a name;
a woman who wandered too far from home.

3. Genealogical

A tree of broken branches,
a trunk of stone,
a season without birds.

4. Phenomenological
From somewhere
not from nowhere;
not from here,
so from there; another there,
not the here we know;
a former here. It exists
because I exist.

5. Quantum Mechanical

Because no one opened the box,
I am still there, and also here.

THE RAPTURE HAS BEEN POSTPONED UNTIL FURTHER NOTICE

Somewhere in Jerusalem, a tree continues to grow.
The seas give up plans to turn blood-red, wave invitingly toward shore.

The locusts, then, are never born.
The weatherman says to plan a beautiful weekend for hiking.

Someone later sees four horsemen in a small-town tavern drinking beer, too
    drunk to speak.
Four horses parked outside, still as a broken carousel.

The omen no one saw gives up and goes back home, heats up a TV dinner,
    and sulks.
The grasses break their fever and can't bring themselves to burn.

The earth suppresses a dangerous quake with a little Pepcid AC and some
    ice cream.
Those who had planned to be raptured instead attend that evening's PTA
    meeting.

Jesus lets his hair grow long and tries to get the band back together.
Bellybuttons vanish.

In Los Angeles, clouds of smog tease themselves apart like cotton, letting
    sunlight through.
The Oscars will be held as previously planned.

A crafty dermatologist lances the last boil, and the boil-afflicted take to the
    streets to dance.
The lepers gather up their extremities and buy up all the units in a foreclosed
    co-op.

The babies once bound for limbo release their bowels and sing.

RESPONSE REQUESTED: SURVEY OF AMERICAN ATTITUDES

There are more or fewer primates in the wild today than there used to be.

There is more or less war in the world than needs to be.

There is more or less shouting in my parents' marriage than I want there to be.

There is more or less sex in my parents' marriage than I want there to be.

There are more or fewer thermonuclear weapons of mass destruction available to dictators than there should be.

There are larger or smaller discounts to be enjoyed at big box retailers than there used to be.

There are more or fewer divorces than there ought to be.

There is more or less graffiti about genitals than there used to be.

There is more or less graffiti than we have good poetry.

There is more or less graffiti than I want there to be.

There are more or fewer millionaires in Congress than I believe there should be.

There are too many or too few saints in the panoply of religion than I believe there should be.

There are far too many or far too few laws outlawing sodomy than our children need.

There are more or fewer murders committed than I've planned this week.

There are more or fewer parties where I'm not a VIP.

There are more or fewer parties than can sustain direct democracy.

There are more or fewer reasons to embrace some form of celibacy.

There are more or fewer people I'm comfortable describing as "hot" or "sexy."

There is more or less nuclear waste for us to store underground.

There is more or less fear of being consumed by a ten-million-degree mushroom cloud.

There are more or fewer airplanes with more or fewer suicide bombers.

There is more or less security, more or fewer patdowns, more or fewer arrests than I believe there should be.

There is more or less underwear worn beneath our clothes than there used to be.

There is more or less alcohol purchased on Ladies' Night than there used to be.

There are more or fewer feral cats making love in the alley than there ought to be.

There are more or fewer prison inmates released by DNA acquittal than I believe
there should be.

There are more or fewer dice in Las Vegas than I need there to be.

There is more or less losing than ever I thought possible.

There is more or less wealth than one person can share.

There is more or less death than any one person can bear.

BUY NOW: HOMES FROM THE LOW $400s

Houses without the moon inside them.
Houses lifting from earth like hot air balloons.
Houses at rest, catching their breath.
Houses festooned with streamers and believers

on the baptism's slow afternoon.
Houses with doors locked up by bolts.
Houses whose colors change with seasons.
Houses with rooms that always feel cold.

Houses belying an eighth deadly sin.
Houses with galaxies within, with dust
and nebulae and comets jammed within.
Houses absolved of all their residents.

Houses resolved of their recurring impediments.
Houses fallen dark, houses gone silent, houses for rent.

TWO HUNDRED CHANNELS AND EVERYTHING'S ON

Seven Marines were killed
today in a bloody confrontation outside

> a new car! This top-of-the-line Ford Focus
> features power windows, power seats, seating for

a family of five earning less than $50,000
now exists below the poverty line, according to

> visits from Ancient Aliens, this week on
> History Channel: history in the making

chocolate chip cookies, y'all! These treats are
my sons' favorite thing about the holidays

> in bus stations and park benches. Home
> foreclosures continue to rise, especially

among Golden Globe nominees this year. With
more on that story, we go to our Hollywood

> Boulevard shooter gunned down after
> spraying gunfire at passing cars earlier this

current slate of Republican candidates can't seem
to make headway among voters, leaving the race

> wide open for Danica Patrick to make her
> play for first place! She powers ahead of

the shuttle Atlantis, manned by a crew of America's
foremost astronauts, including the husband of

Elton John, who spoke on the condition of
anonymity regarding England's phone hacking

group Anonymous unleashed another attack today,
this time targeting Mexican drug cartels, releasing

her fifth number one single from *Teenage Dream*,
tying her with Michael Jackson for the record

of voting against civil rights for gays and lesbians,
including DOMA and the repealed Don't Ask, Don't

squeeze the Charmin! Charmin is softer than
ever before, and leaves fewer pieces behind compared

to the previous season, which saw Ross and Rachel end their
relationship over Ross's ill-timed affair while he claimed

he needed everything in the house: years' worth of
newspapers, tin cans, old clocks, rat feces—the smell

of money drifts down Wall Street where protesters
set up camps, food trucks, even a library of books

will be obsolete by the year 2028. Instead, readers will
download literature directly into their brains via

a connecting flight from Hartford to Dulles, where
travelers hoping to be home for the holidays will be

America's next great fashion designer. Fifteen
designers will be pushed to their limits to create

jobs for working and middle-class Americans.
Congress's approval rating is at the lowest it has

sleeves, warm fleece to wrap around you
so your arms don't get cold while you

fight the insurgents outside Baghdad. The war,
the president said, has finally come to an end.

II.
STORY
PROBLEMS

INSTRUCTIONS TO THE EXAM TAKER

This four-part exam will help you determine if symptoms you experience may be caused by a midlife crisis. This exam is not exhaustive and does not replace or supplant the diagnosis of a trained, licensed psychologist, but it can shed light on feelings and experiences you may find troubling, even if they were natural to you before. There is no treatment for a midlife crisis, just as there is no treatment for adolescence.

Quiz on this section:

    a. Where are you going with your life?

    b. List recent stressful events in the following categories: job changes, death, divorce, major illness, chemical/toxic exposure.

    c. Why are you so angry at society? Provide concrete examples.

    d. When do you most feel trapped or powerless? Follow-up: Are you white?

1. ORIGIN MYTHS

I went out looking for the origin of absence. I knew the universe had a pre-existence but did not consider there to be an absence then. Absence came later. Before there was loss, there was gain. The Big Bang. Debris sailing out for millennia in every direction. Then planets cooled. Then humans.
Now this. When I chart my mother's life, beginning to end, on a timeline of the cosmos, I can't even see the dot. But a universe has been taken from me. Absence, I believe, is older than this.

Quiz on this section:

   a. Have you ever noticed how large an empty sky is and how much nothingness it contains?
   b. Describe the top three hairstyles of the narrator's mother. Use six words or fewer.
   c. How does the narrator's use of the word "loss" differ from your understanding of it?
   d. When was the first time the narrator experienced the burden of self-awareness?

2. THE WATER CYCLE

Mythologies attribute destruction to an elemental force we can't see coming: Fire. Flood. Rivers thick with the red salt of blood. But what about the whisper, the one we make inside the ear of the man we love when we tell him our time together's done? Breath and words a latticework of ruin. Imagine the cloudless sky that makes rain. We don't know why it falls. But then it does. I lay my body down upon a hotel bed and told him though I loved him I could not be with him. There was a desert outside where it never rains, but when it does, it floods. The desert doesn't know what to do with water. So the water rushes away to someone who does.

Quiz on this section:

    a. Identify three grand spiritual narratives alluded to by the narrator in this passage.

    b. Is it more or less difficult to be a homosexual? Be honest.

    c. Draw a diagram of the nitrogen cycle.

    d. Who is the villain of this story, and every story?

3. THE SPACE RACE

The year I was born, NASA launched two probes and set them loose to fly until they died. As far as we know they're still going, now beyond our solar system, now entirely subtracted from our consciousness, now alone. The darkness around them grows deeper and deeper, and I imagine they experience a sense of isolation from everything they have ever known. All they can do is run away from us. And tell me, why wouldn't they? What have we ever done for them? What have *you* ever done for me? I mean, for them.

Quiz on this section:

    a. Point to the most revealing expression in this passage. What does it suggest about you? About me? I mean, the narrator.

    b. Write a diary entry in the voice of a satellite. Date it December 5, 1977.

    c. Sketch the feeling of "isolation" using charcoals or Cray-Pas only.

    d. Describe the atmosphere of a planet in our solar system as though it were your childhood.

4. MEMORY

My family has always curated the Museum of Past Wrongs. Experts now allege it has more exhibits than even the Smithsonian; in fact, there are so many you could visit one each day and never see the whole collection before you die. My wing of the museum is very dark, and I don't like to spend a lot of time in there. It smells faintly of old fruit and basil leaves. For many years I slept in there, among the ruins of myself and everything I thought was true. I'd touch a piece of glass and see my own fingers appear on the other side, so I was never alone.

Quiz on this section:

a. What is your favorite exhibit in the museum described in the passage?
b. Will this narrator ever be able to truly love another human being?
c. Skip this item if you are a resident of the District of Columbia; all others, insert a $5 suggested donation.
d. Describe a place you've visited that was always cold.

5. TEMPORARY DEATH

I've held the hands of two dead bodies in my life. Both of whom I just watched die. Both hands covered with skin translucent as vellum. Veined. Tinged blue. To listen to a human die is an experience I wish I could not describe for you. To watch a loved one breathe out without breathing in makes you stop breathing. There's a long moment that follows in which no one watching is really alive. And then the rest of you go back to living.

Quiz on this section:

    a. What is the narrator's most significant regret?
    b. Identify the key phrase in this section that underpins all the narrator's emotional failings.
    c. Who will hold your hand when you die? Be specific.
    d. Extra credit: make up another word for death. It must have four syllables.

6. IF/THEN STATEMENTS

Many poets and pop singers have written of how people are made of stars. But let's be real: stars are also made of people. Maybe heaven's not so far-fetched; maybe gazing up to "the heavens" isn't so crazy after all. Maybe the people we've loved will be up there—their molecules, their basic chemistry—and maybe someone like Socrates is already there in the glow of a million newborn stars, sending light our way, not a wick of recognition that a star could be anything but a star.

Quiz on this section:

    a. How many stars will you become after you die? Use a decimal instead of a fraction.

    b. Why don't novelists seem to care about the composition of human beings?

    c. If our bodies return to the universe upon our deaths, what happens to the memories we spend our entire lives gathering and cataloging?

    d. Which came first, stars or people? Which will endure longer?

7. MYSTERY AT PLYMOUTH ROCK

When you surround yourself with things, eventually you will become surrounded. This was how the Pilgrims died, some accounts suggest. I have often felt deep down like a pilgrim from another age. When the world around me wasn't strict enough, I wanted to depart. But I never saw myself as doing harm. Here, smallpox blankets. Here, musket balls. Here, white people. Before there were mirrors, I had no idea I was any of these things.

Quiz on this section:

a. Why isn't everyone white, even in their hearts?
b. How many civil wars has America actually fought? Do not estimate.
c. If vertical angles are congruent, how can the distance between two people feel so far?
d. Explain why a race is something you win and something applied to you.

III.
INSTRUCTIONS
FOR USE

INSTRUCTIONS BETWEEN TAKEOFF AND LANDING

First, remain calm. Stow
loose articles in the overhead bin
or the space beneath
the seat in front of you.
Keep necessary in-flight items
like prescriptions and headphones
within easy reach. Command
your bladder to relax. Listen to
the pre-flight instructions. Identify exits.
Identify suspicious passengers.
Identify those who are suspicious of you.
Smile at the flight attendants.
They may need to assist you
in case of an emergency,
and you do not want them to
hate you. Do not be
a douchebag to the person sitting
next to you. Come to an agreement
about the arm rest. Place your feet
somewhere, you know, out of the way.
Remain in your shoes. If you
feel the need to pass gas, please, God,
don't. In the event of turbulence,
hold on to something firm. Do not
hold on to your seat neighbor.
In the event of severe turbulence,
hold your tongue. Do not
scream and kick the seat in front of you.
Do not shout, "Dear God, Dear God,
we're going to die." Do not be caught
praying to your God unless
you really think it's the end.
Do not flail. Do not whimper.
In the event of a water landing,

do not change into your bathing suit.
Do not change into your birthday suit.
Do not change anything about
what you are wearing unless
it is to add more clothing.
Keep your eyes on the exits.
Keep your eyes on suspicious passengers
and crying babies and people
who are praying. They might know
something you don't. Or you may
read a magazine. You may read *SkyMall*,
for instance. Consider purchasing
the litter-box-disguised-as-an-indoor-planter,
for instance. Contemplate your life. But do it
silently. Contemplation does not require
your voice. If you can, try to get
a little sleep. When the plane
begins its descent, you may look
out the window to ensure the plane
doesn't crash. You may stare
right at the fasten seatbelt sign
until it clicks off because then
you will know you haven't died.
You may then unbuckle your seat belt.
You may then reach into carry-on items
within easy reach. You may then thank God
or whomever you want to thank
you survived. You may thank
those suspicious passengers for not
being terrorists. They may even
thank you back. As you deplane,
please do so row by row
in an orderly fashion.
Remain calm. When you step off the plane,
remember to breathe.

HOW TO FALL IN LOVE WITH STRANGERS

Order dinner together.
Enunciate clearly and use
thoughtful language. Draw attention
to your lips. Wear something you know
the other would appreciate.
Undress. Keep
a diary. Imagine life
without each other and how
sad that life would be.
Open a joint bank account,
then make regular deposits. Be frugal
with finances when you must. Pray
together. Pray separately to be
together. Pray the other will just
shut the hell up before you really
lose it. Agree
to disagree. Disagree
frequently. Use eye contact
to communicate your intentions,
then look away. Record the frequency
and quality of your lovemaking sessions
using objective statistics. Thank God
for pretty much everything. Replace empty
rolls of toilet paper without being
told. Surprise each other with small gifts
or weekends out of town. Make a plan
to get each other out of a burning
building should one of you fall
unconscious. Breathe deeply
of each other's scent. Consume
each other's sweat. Establish a shared
vision of the future. Define
"future." Adopt a pet from a shelter
and replace all its sadness with your

love. Keep a tidy house without
being told. Ask for directions when
you are lost without being told. Ask for
help. But not too much
help. Show ample affection. But not too much
affection. Respond to text messages
and phone calls. But maybe you could
wait a little bit. Establish an exercise routine
without being told. Maintain eye contact
in conversations. But not too much
eye contact. That can be
creepy. Don't hold
grudges. Unless you
really have a right to hold that grudge, then
never let it go. Buy a home together
and furnish it with items
neither of you really likes. Forgive.
But always remember what
the other said.

STILL

I find your photo
      in a box where, years ago,
            I buried you just to make you

go away. Your body
      unchanged. You could not have
            imagined how I look now: this

other man's face, his
      skin, his hair thinning. But in-
            side him is a man who loves

who you were, is still
      angry at you for fights otherwise
            forgotten, who hesitates before

he says your name, even
      still, as if speaking the language
            of a country he was born in

but has worked hard
      to forget. On the radio today,
            a woman called in to say her

son died three weeks
      ago, the rawness of her voice
            like cold meat on skin, her

sentence breaking
      like a vase, flooding the radio
            with her grief, which, like

water, fills everyone
      who hears it. I cannot take
            any more pain from other

people's misery.
  Last week, in concert:
    a musician we'd seen

ten years ago. Her face
  aged only around the eyes.
    Where the world enters us

is where it leaves
  its scars. The wounds given
    us are ours to tend alone.

Your suicide was not
  a crime against life. It is
    a limp most people can't
      detect. A lie I always tell.

DEAR AMERICA

A cento of Adrienne Rich

You're beginning to float free
Toward a new kind of love
Burning itself, burning down
The blueprint of a life.

I wanted to choose words that even you
Intend to refuse shelter
With a lie. And each
A beautiful tumor
Feeding on everything.

The words are maps
In a room where too much has happened for you to bear—
Not a map of choices but a map of variations,
Our country moving closer to its own truth and dread.
I know already who wants to buy it, sell it, make it disappear—
You're what the autumn knew would happen
On a grey day of early spring, faint flakes driven.

I came to see the damage that was done.
I want you to see this before I leave
And you must look back.

A conversation begins
In the empty street, on the empty beach, in the desert.

Isn't revolution but a way of knowing
Language cannot do everything.

HOW WIVES SHOULD UNDRESS IN FRONT
OF THEIR HUSBANDS

—After a feature in LIFE *magazine, 1937*

Have something baking.
Remember your husband works hard; he wants to play hard.
Consider the gait of the blue heron.

Establish good posture.
Make light conversation—about the weather, current events.
Think about England.

Begin after coffee and dessert.
Avoid direct eye contact—it can flummox your mate's libido.
Consider the allure of the silver vixen.

Do not think about politics or war.
Do not discuss your chores or what you watched on television.
Picture your body as a bank of fog.

Picture your body as cake.
Picture Botticelli's *The Birth of Venus* or another classical nude.
Consider the humility of the emperor penguin.

Open a dialog with God.
Transcend textiles; evolve beyond shame.
Picture your body as blueprints.

Dissolve into his eyes and mouth.
If time, recite multiplication tables silently to yourself.
Consider the patience of the deathstalker scorpion.

You have been baking all day.
You are a treat he's dreamed of since waking.
Picture your body as an extension of his body.
Consider the lesson of the passenger pigeon.

MERCY

The Dalmatian sank from me
when I set him on the grass,

pausing to kneel before his bones
crumpled away. I knew he was reaching

toward death. I wanted to help him
snatch it in his jaws.

I can trace this moment forward
to the end of so many things:

my address, the life I'd planned,
the man I held until I saw

I was never his. Weeks later,
dog prone on the bed where sunset

gilded him each afternoon, I stroked
his ear's velvet and told him he would

always be my good boy. When it comes
to loss I've learned to tear the limb away

in one quick yank. You can shriek once
or you can cry your whole damned life.

Pain has an echo. I started talking
about a dog but now I'm telling you

how many times I've been a terrorist
whose belief in a better world

blooms only once the stem is cut.

IV.
STORY
PROBLEMS

1. THE PAST

It's already too late when you discover you have done things that cannot be undone. The past is real to us but exists behind a scrim through which our bodies cannot pass. Because we cannot change the past, we can only change ourselves. We are not a sum total of our lived (read: imagined) experiences, are we? (Someone, check on that.) What's in the past can stay buried there, but like all zombies it won't stay buried for long. Some people think the past wants to consume our brains, and I'd agree with that. I'd like to add the past cares little about our pleas.

Quiz on this section:

a. What is more regrettable: asking someone their most regretted memory or hearing their honest reply?
b. If you could change one thing about your past, what would it be and why?
c. List the names of all the men you should have kissed, and the reasons why you didn't.
d. What is your biggest disappointment? Bonus points if that event is still to come.

2. TERRORISTS

The manned mission to Mars will be a one-way trip. But there are a lot of one-way trips in life; I've usually not realized this until I looked back and saw there wasn't a way home. It reminds me of the airport, how once you leave the secure area you can't go back in, no matter what, unless you are a terrorist. You walk through those doors, you look back, you see the only way to return is to cause catastrophe, and then you go on with your life. Maybe it's good some paths have only one direction.

Quiz on this section:

  a. How many things come and go?
  b. Describe three purposeful uses for regret.
  c. Set down this exam and tweet a catalog of your current feelings.
  d. Optional place for a primal scream.

3. PHANTOM PAIN

I never wanted to write again of the rupture between two lovers when their union decays into a rubric of disconnected feelings. Oh, love. You are the sum total of these parts: of sadness, of longing, of joy, of desire, of trust and mistrust, of hope and pride and greed, of vanity, of self-immolation and self-aggrandizing, of promises made or broken, of dreams. To be interlocked with another being. To be withheld from love. To be removed like a limb. Consider how we like to tell the amputee's story of triumph and survival. I'm here to tell you the limb, left behind, has something to say.

Quiz on this section:

    a. Why is this narrator so afraid to admit he is what he is?
    b. When did you first realize you had (or hadn't) gendered this narrator in your mind?
    c. Fill in this blank with all the bullshit you bring to this poem: _____
    d. Continue on the back if you run out of space.

4. HINDSIGHT V. FORESIGHT

Narratives can only be understood backward. When something ends, it makes a new beginning, I think, though I won't really know until later. Unfortunately, death is probably not a beginning, but I am so eager to think so because so many other endings are. I can think of death as the big fat end, or I can imagine what happens after that is just so wonderful no one who goes there thinks to come back and tell me about it. This second theory is the basis of basically every religion.

Quiz on this section:

a. Why is this narrator a terrorist who hates Christianity?
b. Does every new beginning come from some other beginning's end?
c. Retrace your steps today and identify every ending and beginning you encountered.
d. Provide proof of your faith. Attach supporting documentation if needed.

5. JOURNEY TO THE CENTER OF THE EARTH

I remember when my ex-boyfriend died it felt like a tunnel opened up inside me and just kept going—into the floor, down into the earth, into the insides of the earth where we imagine existing all the things we can't bring ourselves to speak. Like the universe, grief is infinite and constantly expanding. I lived in constellations of memories whose designs had no higher meaning then. I cried so much. I cried because my hope was gone. I told people later grief is the absence of hope, but even then I knew it wasn't true. Grief is when you have hope, and then hope leaves you.

Quiz on this section:

    a. What is the volume of the tunnel described in this passage? Use metric or Imperial measures.
    b. Does the reader really care if the narrator cries? Critique this disclosure.
    c. Describe the loss of a child or pet without using the letter *I*.
    d. What is death?

6. CALCULATIONS OF INFINITY

I remember looking at the night sky when I was a teenager. I lay on the back deck, unmoving except for my breath. There were so many stars in that country sky, a smear of shimmering lights. I felt so small. Our lives convince us we are so important, but the night sky undoes all that worry. The universe is endless. You can't even wrap your brain around that, can you? We can't conceptualize endlessness. We just don't have that kind of time.

Quiz on this section:

   a. What should you be doing right now instead of reading this?
   b. Don't you think literature is pretty self-indulgent? I mean, be honest.
   c. Write a one-page character sketch of yourself, the way others see you.
   d. Write a one-page character sketch of yourself, the way you wish you were.

7. PRIVILEGE, CONT.

My skin cannot be removed from me so I must learn to understand it. My skin talks. My skin carries a gun and doesn't get shot. My skin is silk charmeuse. My skin has a credit card that never gets declined. My skin has no limits. My skin is absolute. My skin is a villain whose whereabouts can never be conclusively determined.

Quiz on this section:

a. Explain why heroes wear white when whiteness is problematic.
b. Does the narrator of this passage feel bad about his privilege? Cite examples.
c. Is it possible to separate whiteness from gender, class, sexuality?
d. When did you first realize you were or weren't white?

8. DISCIPL(IN)E AND PU(NI)SH

There is a fable of a man who, because of his actions against the gods, was forced to watch the entirety of his life play out on a stage while he sat in the eighth row, center, unable to move. The man experienced great joy at seeing his childhood enacted, and wistful feelings during his teenage years. And when his adulthood began, he tried repeatedly to stand up and shout directions to the actors, hoping to change things. But he found he had no voice, could not remember common words, and so everything that happened before happened again. When the play passed by his current age, he could no longer watch. He withdrew inside himself and, by the time he died on stage, could not be roused from the fugue state into which he'd sunk.

Quiz on this section:

a. In what ways is this passage a blatant rip-off of contemporary cinema about white men?
b. Who is this "fable" really about? Write a name here: _____
c. What year was the worst year that ever was?
d. Optional place for you to confess whatever you've been keeping buried.

V.
HOVER

SPRING PRAYER

"I own you / said the old feeling."
—Jorie Graham

Picnic, grass.
Cattails stirring muck in spring's breeze.

Blanket, scattered
items, crumbs; the magic light of afternoon

sun, honey
on his skin. We will never be lovers

now, this
day confirms it. Loons on the nearby lake

paddle, coo
that haunting call, like what the heart would

say, should
we ever give it words. I have known his skin's

scent, texture—
stubble as woolen as the blanket we

share; mouth
with a unique, unforgettable taste. But

kisses, skin
aren't the conversation today. Spring around

us, lying
about rebirth, the animals secretly

mating, parting—
they feel no longing, do they.

God, make
me an animal now. Give me this emptiness.

ONLY THIRTEEN BLIMPS REMAIN ON EARTH

For Lillian Matchett

Blimps are the manatees of the sky:
slow, fat, docile.

A group of blimps
is called a *fantasy.*

A wild blimp can travel
two hundred miles a day
with help from kind winds.

Only thirteen blimps remain
on Earth. Surviving blimps
live alone, in captivity.

Blimps seem unafraid of human contact.
Blimps appear in the sky any time of year.
A blimp's largest organ is its one sac lung.

A fantasy of blimps will never again
gather in our sky. The moon
is thought to be jealous of their spectacle.

Blimps are not permitted to mate
with other blimps; they live
a monastic life.

Humans and time are the blimp's only predators.

When a blimp dies, remaining blimps
sense this loss and they, for a short time,
refuse the sky.

We cannot be sure if blimps
believe in heaven.

PENSÉES

After Pascal

When I go for long periods of time without writing, I think I'm washed up, that I did everything I was meant to do, and it wasn't much, and that the usefulness of my life has exhausted itself.

When I feel bored, it feels like what I imagine death feels like: like you can't, no matter what, find something to occupy your mind.

When I go for long periods without dreaming, I wonder what's wrong with me. But then again, when I wake up from vivid dreams, I think, *Jesus Christ, what's wrong with me?*

When people hit on me, I wonder why it's almost always in a completely pornographic and horrifying way. Then I wonder why I'm so Anne of Green Gables when it comes to sex. Then I feel like having sex, but probably not with this person.

When people hit on me but then they say something really vapid about art, it's like that scene in *The Point of No Return* when Harvey Keitel pours acid all over the dead body in the bathtub and it dissolves. Except my penis does that. And sometimes my heart.

When I think about watching my mother die, I get so sad it feels like I sink so deep into my body I'll never be able to claw my way back up to the surface and breathe again.

When I think about what it would be like if my mother were still alive right now, I wonder if she'd like the poems I was writing or if she'd read them and then look at me with that almost confrontational expression and say, *I don't get it.*

49

When I think about my mother, I try to think about the last four years when she was sick and she realized it was time to be happy and, though she didn't say it out loud, I'm pretty sure she thought to herself, *Who the fuck cares now?*

When I think about my mother, I remind myself not to wait until I'm sick to get happy.

When I think about being happy, I often picture myself alone—not because I don't like people, but because I like missing them so much more.

When I think about all the people I've known who've been important to me, I realize I don't talk to many of them anymore, but not because I don't still care for them and remember them. I don't know why it's like this, but it is.

When I think about what I was like when I was younger, I feel embarrassed, but I also try to be forgiving because I was so much stupider then, yet my opinions were louder and stronger than they are now.

When I think about smoking, I feel so glad I quit, and I also think about how wonderful the idea of smoking is.

When I think about my favorite things in life, I realize how many of them work best when you're alone, like playing guitar horribly and playing one-player video games and reading books and running on a treadmill. And then I realize smoking was the only social thing I was ever good at, but it was killing me.

When I think about socializing, it often makes me want a drink, since everyone comments on how much more fun I am after a few cocktails. It often makes me feel like they're right. I am more fun when I've been drinking, and I wonder why I'm not that fun all the time.

When I think about how people see me, I hope they think I'm a nice person, because mostly I am, though I think we're all allowed to be unrepentant assholes about five times in our lives, and I've still got three times left.

When I think about the people who've really hurt me, purposefully and knowingly, I wonder if they will die the horrible deaths I've imagined for them, or if they'll at least be publicly humiliated like characters in a TV sitcom for teenagers.

When I think about humiliation, I think about how jealous I am that Wayne Koestenbaum wrote a whole book about it, and how one night I told Wayne Koestenbaum I loved his red chinos, but he acted like it was kind of an insult, though it was sincere. I love red chinos.

Sometimes I think about New York, and how living there can't possibly be worse than living in Washington, DC, though I can't think of anything worse than living in Washington, DC, again.

Sometimes I think moving to Washington, DC, was a huge mistake because my mother was sick and I should have stayed behind to care for her and even though my job in Phoenix was giving me shingles, it was still better than the job I had in DC.

Sometimes I want so badly to be the kind of person who can rise out of the past like a mist, beautiful and translucent, knowing exactly which direction to move.

Sometimes I wish I were still a kid; plus then I could stop worrying about whether people thought I was gay and just start having sex like every other gay kid I've ever known did.

When I think about the gay guys I know having sex in their early teens, I get sad and jealous because I spent so much of my life being afraid to let myself be myself, and by the time I got around to it, I wonder if it was too late.

Sometimes when I think it's too late, a stranger will say something reassuring to me, which is equally miraculous because strangers often frighten me into silence.

When I think about the kindness of strangers, I feel grateful, and I remind myself to feel grateful more often because gratitude feels good, like pulling on a pair of pants that fit like they were made for you.

When I think about clothes, I want to go shopping, and I wonder how many pairs of denim are too many pairs of denim. I wonder if you know that was a trick question because there's no such thing as too many pairs of denim; denim is classic and timeless and very American, even though it was the uniform of the working class until it became fashionable for everyone.

When I think about America, I feel scared, and sad, and full of privilege I didn't earn, and regretful of said privilege, and I think about the plights of the poor, the Black, the undocumented, the disenfranchised, and I feel so bloated with the arrogance of America I wonder if I'll ever see a day when there is true freedom for all.

When I think about freedom, I feel grateful that time has softened my delivery of opinions and taught me to listen more and speak less.

When I think about listening, I feel relieved. I would almost always rather listen than speak, unless there is a microphone in my hand, at which point I feel full of things to say, especially if there's an audience in front of me.

When I think about public speaking, I feel joy, not dread. I would almost always rather speak in public than have to speak at, like, a dinner party of strangers. Unless someone handed me a microphone at the dinner party and asked me to say a few words. Then I wouldn't shut up, probably.

When I think about bravery, I think about the people in this country who are putting their lives on the line to push justice forward. I think about Ferguson, Baltimore, Atlanta, Chicago, Los Angeles, New York City, Seattle, Portland, Louisville. I think about the names. I think about pulling back the baseboards and confronting the rot we find there. The rot inside ourselves.

When I think about what America needs, I feel certain I don't have all the answers, but I think a good way to enter this conversation is to listen.

When I think about conversations, I am glad we got to have this one. I'm glad I've had a chance to say what's on my mind. Sometimes there's a lot of stuff there. And honestly, sometimes there isn't.

HOSPICE

1. Lift

I lifted my mother's body from the passenger seat—
the notches of her spine, her slats of ribs—
each bone against my skin, her weight
pulling me down even as I lifted her

my only thought
don't let go
don't let go
don't let go

2. Mortality

The hospice nurse with his close-trimmed beard
skinned with moonlight's milksheen
helping me place her in a wheelchair

I find the solitary gray on his face
We are all dying

3. Ghosts

We pushed her to the room in which she'd die
so clean and somber
we were fooled out of imagining
the last family to cry where we sat

For that
we had nothing but
gratitude

4. Breath

She scooped again and again into her wet lungs

like a fish
tasting air
and hating it

5. Nature

The desert drowns in sheets of rain
because it cannot take in
this bounty

Is it stubborn
or just dumb

6. Questions

I held her hand
Her cold fingers white-blue
I looked into her face
I wanted more time
I wanted to know she was safe
These were the things I could not have now or ever
It was mid-morning
We asked the clock for more specifics

7. Hospice (Detail)

Everyone in hospice continued toward
oblivion, but in our room all was stopped

Her breathing—our breathing

8. The Weight I Carried

I let it fall. I waited so long
to hear it land

for that sound
when I would know the weight
touched down

It never came

9. Breath (Later)

Her post-it notes
throughout the house

each one flapping
in the unseen breath
of ceiling fans.

VI.
STORY
PROBLEMS

1. EULOGIES FOR HOME

My mother has died. It still feels odd to know that. It seems somehow impossible it can be true. The body that made my body has been burned to ash and sits in a box. But still I can hear her voice. Could I have remembered each moment with her better, like an etching I could not brush away—or is the slow progression of forgetting a blessing? Imagine you walk from a house across a long expanse, turning to look back every few hours. The house retreats from you, grows smaller, no longer smells like you, forgets you. After some time, it will vanish from you, too. We give each other this mutual oblivion as a kind of final gift.

Quiz on this section:

a. Draw from memory the floor plan of the first house you lived in.
b. Why is death so, I don't know, final?
c. If the dead could communicate with us, what do you think they'd want to talk about?
d. Do you believe in ghosts of unfamous people?

2. THE LIGHTNING STRIKE IN THE FIELD OF ABANDONED CARS

Between age twelve and twenty-three, I thought about crying, but it was an abstraction, something other people did, something awkward and unfortunate. Then my heart was wrecked like a hundred-year-old tree limb coming down in a storm. You could hear the crack of it for miles. I cried for three days. Now that I think of it, I'm not sure I ever really stopped. I had a lot to make up for. Now I'm like some kind of myth.

Quiz on this section:

a. If Replicants can cry, why aren't they human? Or at least *human enough*?
b. If a human cannot cry, explain how they are honestly no longer human.
c. Experiment: taste the tears of the next person you see crying. Critique the flavor.
d. Recall a time you couldn't wait to forget.

3. MISERY: AN OCEANOGRAPHY

It's natural to feel curiosity about the depth of human misery. How deep does it go? When a tragedy occurs, you may think, *This—this is the absolute worst I will ever feel.* There's an optimism that follows. This will only improve, and things can never be this bad again. Except that depth was not the bottom. We cannot see—at least, not yet—into the deepest crevasses of our oceans, or the things that live there. Misery is a lot like that. We all know it exists. And we can be sure something—something—is alive inside. That it is hungry.

Quiz on this section:

a. Isn't this a lot of scientific hoo-ha we can disprove through simple Bible study?
b. Express the temperature of the ocean's greatest depth as a function of color.
c. If hunger is a predictor of misery, explain the role of starvation in survival.
d. What even is this?

4. THE TAUTOLOGIST IN LOVE

I am not very old, but I have cataloged no fewer than six types of romantic love in my life. I am not a skilled researcher to say the least, nor have I been a conscientious student of the experience. However, I hypothesize at least seventeen other types of romantic love may exist, both here and on other planets, though the average person will never know more than twelve. To know too many variations of love is maddening. The human brain can only master so many languages. To ask more of it is inviting the kind of disaster I just can't write about here.

Quiz on this section:

   a. It is the year 2057 and humankind has evolved into speaking a single language. Please write their word for love in this blank: _____
   b. If the narrator of this section were the flag of an existing nation, which nation would that be and why?
   c. Can you trust someone who claims to know six types of romantic love? Why or why not?
   d. True or false: marriage is a form of poetry complete with restrictions and many failed examples.

5. DISSECTION

For a time, I believed people could hear my thoughts. How else did they know my most private desires, the reluctance in my heart when I looked too long at a boy in my class? There was no privacy then. I remember the anatomical model in biology class, the clear skin whose organs, color-coded, could be removed for study. The way the children tore each one out and tossed them back and forth, laughing, disgusted. I wanted their freedom, the way they never needed to learn anything about themselves.

Quiz on this section:

    a. Briefly explore the difference between the terms "public" and "private."
    b. Write down the names of three people you victimized as a child.
    c. Why has God forsaken his children? (Atheists only: Why have you forsaken God?)
    d. If freedom isn't free, calculate its unit cost based on the information in the passage.

6. THE PROGNOSIS WAS NEVER GOOD

I never envied my mother more than when I saw her liberated from her own expectations, when she was terminal. I remember as a child thinking she was perfect, then thinking she was flawed when I'd grown out of it. I sprained my ankle when I was three—how is not important. But for weeks after, she had to carry me everywhere, propped on her hip. I was a miserable kid. I think that's why we loved each other.

Quiz on this section:

    a. What is your earliest memory of physical injury?
    b. If you could be any animal, living or extinct, what would it be and why?
    c. Why is the narrator thinking of his childhood in this passage?
    d. Why does regret taste like vinegar?

7. SECRET IDENTITY

I try not to look at old photographs of myself. I can see that boy is dying. I can see the way his mask almost doesn't fit, the uncanny slipping of his false face away from his true face. He had so much hair. He had all his teeth. People would look at him and think nothing inside of him had ever been broken, but they were mostly wrong. People can live for years on the edge of ruin like that. People can live for years until they realize they're gone.

Quiz on this section:

    a. Is this getting depressing yet? Why or why not?

    b. Write a letter to this narrator's younger self. Apologize for what he's going to do.

    c. Why do we allow others to name us when no one knows us better than ourselves?

    d. Go back through this entire book and underline meaningful passages, then throw it away.

8. THE SPACE RACE, CONT.

Voyager 2's only task is to observe. It has traveled to places humans could once only imagine, then could only see through powerful telescopes. Voyager 2 carries within it—I'll just say it—a great deal of humankind's hope. The Mozart, the messages. The greatest achievements in human history like music and optimism. It's a beautiful thing the way we cast it away from Earth and into oblivion. What a brave soldier it is. The only testament we have from both science and faith.

Quiz on this section:

    a. Do we become more or less optimistic the more we learn about the universe?
    b. What will happen when the universe stops expanding?
    c. What will happen to you when the universe stops expanding?
    d. What will happen at the end that does not give birth to a beginning?

9. THE NIHILIST'S GAMBIT

Pascal said, basically, *If you believe, you can get into heaven. If there's no heaven, you've lost nothing. If there is a heaven, you win. If you don't believe and there is a heaven, you lose.* It seems fair enough. But the older I've gotten, the less I want to hold out for heaven. I pray for oblivion, complete dissolution, absolute destruction of myself. Erasure. I want to believe death is final-final. That everyone I've lost hasn't elected to stay gone. That when I go, I'll carry nothing forward.

Quiz on this section:

    a. Why are humans so trusting of the printed word?
    b. If you could convince the people who love you of a single lie, what would it be?
    c. Imagine religion is a choice, not something applied to you, like your name. Oh, wait.
    d. Why wouldn't you want to die?

VII.
LANDING

MORTALITY

I still might die before I get much older than this.

I still might die before the dog dies, even though she ages at a rate of approximately five years for every year I age; she tends to be more careful than me: she barks at danger, has quick reflexes.

I still might die before you die, love, so really, we should get out and do something fun today instead of spending our time on our computers across the same room from each other.

I still might die before Halley's Comet comes back around.

I still might die before my nemesis gets what's coming to him.

I still might die before we move out of this godforsaken hellhole and into a nice place, somewhere our plants don't die after two weeks.

I still might die before I see a volcano.

I still might die before we get to Six Flags Over Georgia.

I still might die but maybe you won't die, so I want you to know right now you shouldn't feel bad the first time you have sex with someone else. I'm rooting for you.

I still might die by shark attack, my greatest fear!

I still might die in a plane crash, my second greatest fear.

I still might die in a home accident, the most common location of personal injuries.

I still might die in my Scion. Please, God, don't let me die in a Scion.

I still might die at yoga, so at peace with myself even my heart lies still in Shavasana. I still might die in the shape of Shavasana—corpse pose.

I still might die and have my death made into a Lifetime TV movie I know you will ultimately watch over and over.

I still might die and the movie they make about my life might be called *Mother, May I Sleep with Danger Part II.*

I still might die on a boat, in a cab, on a bicycle, on a skateboard, on a public bus, in a limousine, in the SuperShuttle on the way to an airport, or in a rickshaw.

I still might die in a rickshaw, but the chances are pretty slim at this point.

I still might die in Asia or at Asian Bistro, the closest I've ever come to visiting Asia. I still might die in Italy or at Leaning Tower of Pizza while eating lasagna.

I still might die like Mama Cass, choking on a hoagie.

I still might die like Elvis, sitting on the can.

I still might die like Judy Garland, drunk and sitting on the can.

I still might die like James Dean, in a car wreck I totally saw coming.

I still might die in a car crash, which probably wouldn't surprise anyone who's ever been a passenger in my Scion.

I still might die of tuberculosis.

I still might die of AIDS, cancer, flesh-eating virus, a bowel obstruction, an embolism, an aneurism, a stroke, a bloody nose I can't control, a perforated ulcer, gangrene, scurvy, sepsis, multiple sclerosis, non-Hodgkin's lymphoma, Lou Gehrig's disease, hepatitis C, jaundice, liver failure, kidney failure, arsenic poisoning, an undetected heart abnormality that has been silently ticking away like a bomb inside my chest, or bird flu.

I still might die before I visit Legoland (in Denmark, not California).

I still might die like Joyce Summers on *Buffy the Vampire Slayer*, and you'll come home and find me on the couch but I won't be breathing, and you'll try to save me but you won't be able to.

I still might die and come back to life like the vampire in the morgue at the end of that episode—I doubt it, but I still might.

I still might die before I have destroyed every copy of Stephenie Meyer's *Twilight* I can find.

I still might die before I ever get around to reading *Dune*.

I still might die before I finish writing another book that is better than *Twilight* but shorter than *Dune*.

I still might die before I finally clean off my desk.

I still might die while being forced to observe Daylight Saving Time.

I still might die in the Grand Canyon, which I won't mind unless it is by falling from a great height, in which case it would be my third most-feared way to die.

I still might die by stabbing, which I am also very afraid of dying by. The thought of something puncturing my body makes me unbearably sad.

I still might die in a robbery gone wrong.

I still might die by friendly fire.

I still might die doing one last job before I get out of the business for good.

I still might die before I figure out where I put my savings bond.

I still might die before retirement age, in which case all that saving will have been for nothing. Nothing!

I still might die before my dad dies, but I don't know which is sadder: watching your child die or living without the people who made you.

I still might die before I get a chance to have a baby; you once told me, "You should definitely reproduce," which I thought was a really sweet thing to say.

I still might die before you like it and you finally put a ring on it.

I still might die before we register at Target.

I still might die before we go to Hawaii, which is where I'm hoping you might take me on a honeymoon before I die.

I still might die before I go surfing again, which was probably one of the best times I've had even though the entire time I was praying I would not be eaten by a shark.

I still might die before I see Chris Isaak in person again, although he will probably never look as good as he did the first time I saw him and got his autograph and swooned so visibly and so forcefully I almost passed out like someone in *Gone with the Wind*.

I still might die before I see Gwyneth Paltrow shopping in LA.

I still might die before I see Sarah Michelle Gellar shopping in LA.

I still might die before I see another Pedro Almodóvar movie.

I still might die before I make it to the moon.

I still might die while buried alive, which actually doesn't scare me as much as it should or as much as shark attack, plane crash, or stabbing do, and I still might feel secretly relieved to finally have a few minutes to myself before I die.

I still might die like my Uncle Charlie, who was a big practical joker and used to leave fake dog poop and whoopee cushions around the house, and who was so funny that when he went into convulsions after dinner everyone thought he was joking around and laughed at him the whole time, and then let him lie silently in the chair while chiding him for taking it too far, and then only realizing he was dead when the dinner party broke up and everyone went home and someone tried to "wake" him.

I still might die while I'm on a diet.

I still might die before I reach my goal weight.

I still might die before I feel like I have a truly beach-worthy body.

I still might die feeling a certain degree of self-loathing or, short of that, self-disappointment.

I still might die before I own a home.

I still might die before we have a backyard for the dog.

I still might die before I figure out how to plant flowers and then keep them alive.

I still might die before I learn to appreciate seafood, but I will definitely die before I ever put shellfish in my mouth, except for shrimp, which I am slowly becoming okay with.

I still might die before I make up for everything I did wrong.

I still might die before I figure out what I did to make a couple of people stop speaking to me.

I still might die before a couple of other people realize I stopped speaking to them.

I still might die earlier than my grandmother, who lived to be 104 and, even though she told me for fifteen years she was about to die, was one of the healthiest people I knew.

I still might die without tasting all the different varieties of wine out there, like a good Malbec, because I would rather drink the wine I already know I like than risk wasting $10 on something I'll pour down the sink in a huff.

I still might die before I visit a dentist again.

I still might die before I get that suspicious mole removed.

I still might die without tan lines, which is probably what my dermatologist would recommend, if I had one.

I still might die before I master the art of French cooking.

I still might die before we remember what it's like not to worry about paying the rent.

I still might die before we have a full-size washer and dryer again, and I still might die before we live somewhere those appliances don't sit in our galley kitchen.

I still might die before we finally take all that old crap to Goodwill.

I still might die before somebody buys some of that old crap we took to Goodwill.

I still might die before anyone reveals who really shot JFK.

I still might die before the first reliable sighting of Elvis.

I still might die before someone traps the Loch Ness Monster, if she exists, and I still might die before anyone figures out why there's water on Mars since there's nobody there to be thirsty or dirty.

I still might die before Voyager 2 is discovered by intelligent life, who scoff at our gold record with its recordings of hello in many languages and some Beatles music.

I still might die before we learn whether or not aliens can get into the Beatles.

I still might die before Nicolas Cage destroys the Freemason cult once and for all!

I still might die without being able to watch another Tom Hanks movie without feeling emotionally manipulated.

I still might die before I see another man naked in real life, which is okay by me.

I still might die feeling lonely, even though I know you love me.

I still might die at a Starbucks location.

I still might die because my love for donuts is really inappropriate.

I still might die because we don't have enough money to buy organic meats and produce.

I still might die because we unknowingly eat genetically modified food, like tomatoes engineered to grow more cubelike so there is less wasted space in the containers when they are shipped to grocery stores.

I still might die without having visited all fifty states, even though I crossed off Alaska and Hawaii— two of the furthest and most expensive to reach.

I still might die without even driving through Wyoming, Idaho, Montana, South Dakota, Arkansas, Rhode Island, Vermont, New Hampshire, or Maine.

I still might die without seeing Connecticut, since I slept through it.

I still might die without honor.

I still might die saving someone else's life from an out-of-control bus, a speeding train, a crazed gunman in a bank, a wild boar attack, an atom bomb blast, a collapsing building, black ice, or a meteorite barreling toward earth.

I still might die before Tom Cruise comes out.

I still might die before John Travolta comes out.

I still might die before somebody deprograms Katie Holmes, which is sad because I sort of liked her.

I still might die before Jake Gyllenhaal seduces me—in my dreams.

I still might die before Hollywood stops making sequels, remakes, and/or reboots.

I still might die before I see *The Rocky Horror Picture Show* at a midnight movie.

I still might die wearing fishnets at a screening of *The Rocky Horror Picture Show*.

I still might die while playing the role of Columbia or Magenta, although I'm really more of a Brad.

I still might die after doing television commercials for medication to treat herpes, erectile dysfunction, overactive bladder, restless leg syndrome, or yeast infections.

I still might die before they invent a pill that makes you happy without leaving you sad.

I still might die before I need to stop wanting a pill that makes you happy without leaving you sad. Or impotent.

I still might die with a computer full of unpublished manuscripts, like Emily Dickinson (minus the computer).

I still might die like Walt Whitman, completely misjudged and underappreciated in my time.

I still might die like James Merrill—rich but sad.

I still might die like Robert Lowell—complicated and sad.

I still might die like John Berryman—sad and falling at a great speed from a high bridge, which is a significant fear of mine (see above).

I still might die like Sylvia Plath—accidentally but leaving behind a book that changes the lives of many other people.

I still might die like Anne Sexton—beautiful and jealous and sad.

I still might die like River Phoenix or Heath Ledger, although it might first imply that my genius had actually been recognized instead of merely imagined (by me).

I still might die like the character Jake Gyllenhaal played in *Brokeback Mountain*—beaten to death for being gay.

I still might die like Shirley MacLaine's character in *The Children's Hour*—struck by a falling tree, for being gay.

I still might die like Robert Downey, Jr.'s character in *Less Than Zero*—from an overdose after giving, like, a ton of blowjobs to rich white guys in Palm Springs, for being gay.

I still might die like any number of real people who were killed for being gay.

I still might die fighting for my life.

I still might die while listening to my iPod, which wouldn't be so bad.

I still might die while taking a phone call.

I still might die while picking up my dry cleaning, my last great extravagance.

I still might die while redeeming a coupon at Express, which is the only time I shop there, and which I haven't done in quite some time, so maybe this is not very likely.

I still might die while taking the dog for a walk.

I still might die and not have an afterlife, in which case I probably won't be feeling much of anything.

I still might die and go to heaven, which would be pretty cool, unless we have to sit around on clouds all day playing harps, in which case I might not bother.

I still might die and go to hell, which I mostly don't believe in because living on earth is usually punishment enough.

I still might die and go to purgatory for a shower of fire that will burn away all my sins.

I still might die and end up in Limbo, which I've been told is *not* where the limbo was invented.

I still might die like that guy who died at Town Danceboutique, on the dance floor, dancing in a sea of little twinks to the thumping insistence of Top 40 pop music. All I can hope is that he died happy doing something he loved, and that I might too.

I still might die and receive a Darwin Award on my way out.

I still might die on a motorcycle, although I've successfully avoided riding one for over twenty years.

I still might die feeling like this.

I still might die wrapped in the stench of rotten food and failure, slumped in a big city alley wearing clothes I can't remember putting on, because I'd put them on so long ago.

I still might die while having sex, which is probably my most hoped-for way to die.

I still might die having the best sex of my life, which seems fair.

I still might die in that shiny, shimmery calm after sex when our sweaty bodies fall onto the bed next to each other and just try to absorb everything about that moment. That might kill me one of these times. That would be okay.

I still might die before I figure out how to get happy.

I still might die, sure. But I still might die happy.

VIII.
STORY
PROBLEMS

1. PARABLE OF THE WHALE

At midlife I drowned in myself. Imagine I am a sea of experiences, memories, hopes, desires. You cannot stop the whale that lives inside. So I went like Jonah into the whale, or like Pinocchio—yes, just a boy, really—a victim, and I lit a fire there; it was so dark inside. And the whale I knew was made of muscle and bone I generated by every choice I ever made. I could not get out of the whale. I could not get out of myself. If this is what you call a "crisis."

Quiz on this section:

    a. Why is masculinity such a meaningless performance?
    b. With what fuel did the narrator start the fire in this passage? (Hint: his tongue)
    c. Where are the emergency exits located?
    d. [Intentionally left blank]

2. DARWIN'S RAZOR

The worst it ever was, I wanted to die. Not for revenge, not because of pain, not because of sadness. I couldn't uncover another escape. At fifteen I checked out a book from my town's little library about suicide techniques. The seventy-five-year-old librarian stamped that card, handed it to me, told me to say hi to my parents. What did she think, later that night, about the teenage boy with the book about death? Who appeared in her dreams, what was he wearing, what did he say to her, how could she live with herself?

Quiz on this section:

  a. Describe the emotion of the narrator based on his facial expression alone.
  b. Replay this section but mute the sound. When burdened with images, what visual metaphors stand out to you?
  c. Recommend two contemporary directors who would succeed in adapting this memory into a feature-length film. Please provide contact information.
  d. Suggest a memory of your own to replace the narrator's memory.

3. FORESIGHT V. HINDSIGHT

Every language has a word for "hello" and for "goodbye." But only English wants to welcome you with *hell* and surrender you with *good*. I suppose an optimist would love this; things will only get better. Does it get better? I mean—what is better? Or are we all just solitary planes holding steady at our altitude until rocked by a trapdoor of turbulence? That whole time we're flying, we know we can only go down. There is a point in our lives when things will never get any better. But we never know it when we're there. Only when we were.

Quiz on this section:

a. Imagine you are the narrator's psychologist. Which medicines would you prescribe? Do not use generic names.
b. Touch a place you dislike on your body.
c. Is hell really that bad? Cite scholarly research using MLA format.
d. If Americans want to speak English, should they go back to England?

4. THEOCRACY AND ITS DISCONTENTS

The discovery of life on other planets will destroy many religions. This seems a foregone conclusion, the way religious texts speak only of Earth, of earthlings, of our hopes and fears, of our punishments and rewards. What gods will these other beings worship? The god of suspicion, the god of musculature, the god of mute creatures, the god of space dust. I could go on. I have a lot of ideas about this. I think the real question is whether or not those gods will speak to us, accept us as their own, if we'll be smart enough to let them.

Quiz on this section:

    a. Do you believe in intelligent life on other planets? What about on this one?
    b. Identify a potential otherworldly god here: _____
    c. Does prayer work, or is it merely the power of positive thinking?
    d. Does thinking work, or is it merely the power of an all-seeing deity?

5. IF WE'RE BEING HONEST

Honesty is not an objective element. It has no mass or velocity. It is not a stone. It is not a bird, though it can fly away from you in silence, how a bat moves in darkness with its dizzied looping but intense quiet. Honesty does not grow on trees. It will not save you from drowning. You cannot exchange it for goods or services. And yet. I'm the kind of person who cannot tell a lie. This statement, in fact, is a bald-faced lie.

Quiz on this section:

>   a. I've really had it with this narrator. What about you?
>   b. Did dragons ever exist and, if so, do you think they were a fairly honest sort?
>   c. What is the periodic symbol for Honesty? Do you think it's more of an alkali metal or a noble gas?
>   d. There is no molecule that spells "honesty." Explain why this might be.

6. SUPERSTITION

My mother knew dropped silverware meant guests would stop by the house. That when my nose itched, I was destined to kiss a fool. And my itchy palms meant money was making its way toward me. Ladybugs always brought good news, but a hat left on the bed invited bad luck. The only thing we feared were birds. When one found its way into our house, it meant a man would die. At fifteen, I found a robin dancing behind the glass door of the fireplace. I could not let it in, couldn't set it free. I was only a child. I wasn't ready to leave.

Quiz on this section:

> a. Would Darwin consider this an example of survival of the fittest?
> b. Prove in syllogism that the only difference between superstition and tradition is fear.
> c. Explain how knowing something is true does not make it true.
> d. Who was the last fool you kissed?

7. COMPASSION

Even as I care for my dog, I accept her death is inevitable. Every one of our days—the happy days, the angry days, the sick days when I cradled her close to my chest in the hopes I'd be well again, and the days we drove in the car for hours just to see where we'd be—wore the shadow of a future sadness that grew darker the more I loved her. I think this is why what we love must die. Love, grown so large, is a shawl of heavy chains. We have two choices: collapse under its weight, or

Quiz on this section:

    a. Why was the author unable to complete this section with words?
    b. Write a brief essay about a pet you once loved. If you've never owned a pet, imagine a pet you once loved. Make sure not to use the pet's name anywhere in the essay.
    c. Calculate the number of stars that perished in the time you took to calculate the number.
    d. Is extinction always bad?

8. THE UNKNOWN UNKNOWNS

No one really knows what lies beyond the solar system, so that's why the twin Voyagers were launched. It took nearly 40 years to reach the farthest corner of the known universe, and now they are moving into uncharted territory. In 2025, they will no longer have the energy to power a single instrument, the way a sick, old body might shut down, system by system, leaving the brain and heart for last. The body is programmed to persevere. Even though it knows it's sailing toward oblivion.

Quiz on this section:

    a. Articulate three distinct differences between bodies and machines.
    b. Do you fear sentient robots? Why not?
    c. Explain what Voyager 1 will discover in 2024. Use diagrams.
    d. Calculate the day and time of your own death using Voyager's formula.

9. IN CONCLUSION

I'm not sure if the origin of absence remains unfound or if it's been repeatedly found and simply absorbed by the souls who discover it. Are they part of the absence now? Or is absence our only shared destiny? I shouldn't ask questions here; they're either rhetorical (needless) or unanswered (uninformative), and what you want from me are solutions. You've come to worry about being lost the way I am lost. I have become a cautionary tale. It's like I begged to become a laurel tree but no one was there to listen. And so what happens at the end came to happen.

Quiz on this section:

    a. Discredit the witness in three steps.
    b. Why is *caution* such an ugly word? Why isn't it an ugly word? Choose a side.
    c. Translate the passage into another language. Extra credit: invent the language.
    d. Optional place for you become the narrator of these passages.

Acknowledgments

I am grateful to the editors of these publications in which these poems previously appeared, sometimes in a slightly different form or with a different title.

Academy of American Poets/Poets.org. "Poem in which Words Have Been Left Out."

American Poetry Review. "Response Requested: Survey of American Attitudes," "Only Thirteen Blimps Remain on Earth."

Assaracus. "The Water Cycle," "Memory," "Mystery at Plymouth Rock," "The Space Race," "Journey to the Center of the Earth," "The Tautologist in Love," "Darwin's Razor," "Foresight v. Hindsight," "Eulogies for Home," and "Secret Identity" from *Story Problems.*

Catamaran Literary Reader. "How Wives Should Undress in Front of Their Husbands," "Instructions between Takeoff and Landing."

DIAGRAM. "The Space Race, Cont.," "The Prognosis Was Never Good," "The Past," "Parable of the Whale," and "The Unknown Unknowns" from *Story Problems.*

The Good Men Project. "Spring Prayer."

Impossible Archetype. "Still."

The Journal. "Two Hundred Channels and Everything's On."

The Laurel Review. "Pensées."

Ocho. "Mortality."

Poet Lore. "How to Fall in Love with Strangers."

Smartish Pace. "A Stranger Asks Where I Am From."

Stirring. "Hospice."

Terrain.org. "Dear America."

Waxwing. "The Rapture Has Been Postponed Until Further Notice."

Whale Road Review. "Buy Now: Homes from the Low $400s."

Zócalo Public Square. "Mercy."

Story Problems won the 2017 Palooka Press Chapbook Prize and was published as a limited-edition chapbook.

I would like to thank members of my community for advice, support, and feedback that shaped this manuscript and helped bring it into the world:

Michael McKeown Bondhus, Gerald Carlin, RJ Gibson, Martín Hernández, Matthew Hittinger, Katie Manning, and Lou Mathews. I am grateful to Mary Biddinger at the University of Akron Press for giving this manuscript a warm and supportive home, and to her colleagues Thea Ledendecker and Amy Freels for shepherding it into the world. I would also like to thank my colleagues and community at UCLA Extension and the Writers' Program for providing an environment conducive to creativity and innovation, especially Ashley, Bree, Carrie, Chae, Jeff, Jennie, Nutschell, and Pascale.

"Dear America" includes lines from the following poems by Adrienne Rich: "Dreamwood," "What Kind of Times Are These," "Yom Kippur 1984," "A Valediction Forbidding Mourning," "Burning Oneself Out," "Cartographies of Silence," "Diving Into the Wreck," "For the Dead," "From an Atlas of the Difficult World," "November 1968," "Prospective Immigrants Please Note," "Victory," "For the Record," and "Implosions."

Notes on *Story Problems*

Question d. of "4. Memory" alludes to a line from the 1986 film *Ferris Bueller's Day Off*, in which Ferris describes his friend Cameron's house as being "like a museum: it's very cold, and you're not allowed to touch anything."

Question a. of "2. Terrorists" references a line from the 1983 song "Karma Chameleon" performed by Culture Club. It was written by George O'Dowd (Boy George), Jon Moss, Mikey Craig, Roy Hay, and Phil Pickett. It peaked at number one on the Billboard Hot 100. Boy George has said the song is about feelings of alienation.

"4. Hindsight V. Foresight" alludes to a quote from Søren Kierkegaard: "Life can only be understood backwards; but it must be lived forwards." Question b. references a line from the 1998 song "Closing Time" performed by Semisonic. It was written by Dan Wilson. It peaked at number eleven on the Billboard Hot 100. Mr. Wilson has acknowledged it is a song many people know but not everyone likes.

Question a. of "8. Discipl(in)e and Pu(ni)sh" alludes to the 2008 film *Synecdoche, New York*, written and directed by Charlie Kaufman, which critics said was either "self-indulgent" or "one of the best films of the decade," as though it couldn't simultaneously be both.

The term "Replicant" in question a. of "2. The Lightning Strike in the Field of Abandoned Cars" is taken from the 1982 neo-noir science fiction film *Blade Runner*, adapted by Hampton Fancher and David Peoples from the Philip K. Dick short story "Do Androids Dream of Electric Sheep?" and directed by Ridley Scott. In the film, investigators known as Blade Runners put subjects through a series of psychological tests to determine if they are human or Replicant, a sophisticated android that is almost imperceptibly different from humans.

"2. Darwin's Razor" alludes to Occam's Razor, which suggests that among competing hypotheses, the one with the fewest assumptions should be considered, but is often paraphrased as "the simplest answer is the correct answer." It is attributed to William of Ockham (1287–1347).